The Littlest Kangaroo

A Story to Share with Your NICU Baby

Jen and Jeremy Moore

illustrated by

Lola Lawrence

I0139782

Copyright © 2025 by Jennifer and Jeremy Moore

All rights reserved. No part of this book may be reproduced, stored in a retrieval system, or transmitted in any form or by any means—electronic, mechanical, photocopying, recording, or otherwise—without the prior written permission of the publisher, except in the case of brief quotations used in reviews, articles, or educational materials.

For information, contact:

Jennifer Moore

Email: Jen@raisingspecialhumans.com

Website: raisingspecialhumans.com

Illustrated by Lola Lawrence

ISBN: 979-8-9992136-0-0

Printed in the United States of America

First Edition

Disclaimer: This book is intended to provide encouragement, comfort, and general information for parents and caregivers of NICU babies. It is not a substitute for medical advice, diagnosis, or treatment from qualified healthcare professionals. Always seek the advice of your physician or other qualified health provider with any questions you may have regarding your child's care.

Dedication

For the doctors and medical staff of Neonatal Intensive Care Units - especially those at Kettering Health Main Campus and Cincinnati Children's Hospital Medical Center. Thank you for the extraordinary care, compassion, and expertise you gave so selflessly each day. You are true angels on Earth. We are forever grateful.

For Caleb and Owen. Thank you for all you have taught us, and for the boundless love and joy you have brought to our lives. We are endlessly proud of you. We love you more than words can express, sweet boys. With all our love, Mom & Dad.

For Lola's children: Reed, Jojo, and Anne-Marie. I love you for everything you are. You have taught me so much, and I am blessed to be your mom.

For our families. Thank you for the countless ways you put your lives on hold when our babies arrived too soon. Your unwavering love, support, and presence not only carried us through those fragile early days, but continue to shape the strong, resilient young people they are becoming. We are endlessly appreciative.

For NICU families everywhere. Wishing you strength, comfort, and hope. You are not alone. We are cheering you on every step of the way. God Bless.

As I sit here skin-to-skin

with my little kangaroo,

I cannot help but dream about

all that we might do.

One day we could make blanket forts,

take walks or play pretend,

read books on lazy afternoons,

then laugh until day's end.

Perhaps you'll be a baseball star,

even score a winning run.

I'm already your biggest fan,

and our journey's just begun!

Peace

Roo for President

Maybe you'll be President,

make a difference,
big or small.

'Till then, I'll be the voice
you need.

I'll catch you if you fall.

You could become a doctor
who heals with hands and heart,
helping little fighters just like you
get their strongest start.

Maybe you'll love nature,

even rocket to the moon.

For right now you are safe, My Dear,

in our shared NICU cocoon.

You could express yourself
in many ways,

that make the world
a better place.

Right now, life's a marathon

and you, Love,
set the pace.

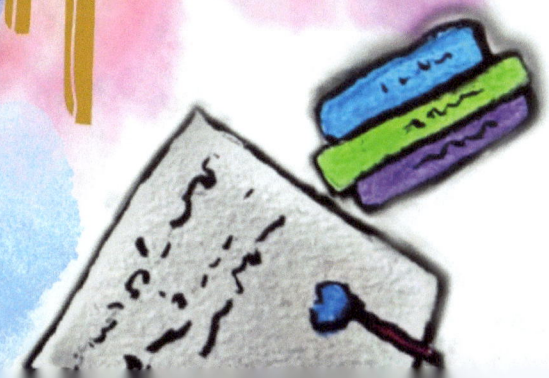

Perhaps you will teach other kids

to be open-minded, too.

Never underestimate the power

of what inclusive hearts can do.

One day we may admire

how you grow so big and tall,

though right here in this moment

you are oh-so-very small.

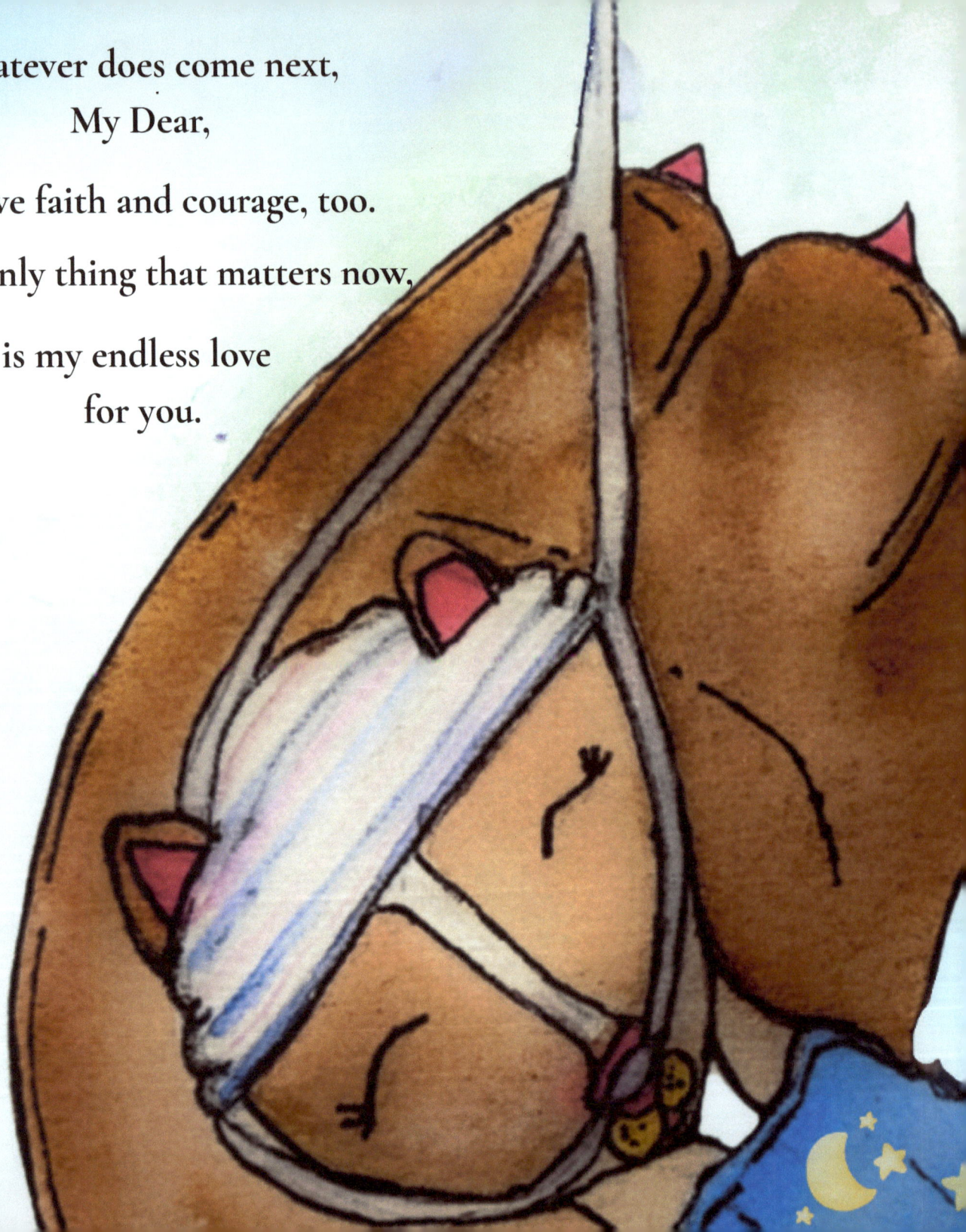

Whatever does come next,
My Dear,

we'll have faith and courage, too.

For the only thing that matters now,

is my endless love
for you.

It's so much fun to hope and dream
of all that we might do,
but for right now we'll sit skin-to-skin:
Me, and my Little Kangaroo.

Kangaroo Care
A Gift of Love and Comfort

What is Kangaroo Care?

Kangaroo Care is holding your baby skin-to-skin—your baby resting on your bare chest, close enough to hear your heartbeat. It is one of the most meaningful ways to support your baby in the NICU. The term comes from the way kangaroo mothers carry their joeys safely in their pouches.

When can Kangaroo Care happen?

Every baby is different. Your NICU care team will help determine the best times and safest ways to practice Kangaroo Care. Even brief periods of skin-to-skin contact can provide comfort and support healing.

Who can participate?

Kangaroo Care is beneficial for both preterm and full-term babies. Parents and guardians can all share in these moments of closeness and connection.

What Does Kangaroo Care Do?

Helps your baby feel safe and warm

Your body helps your baby stay at a comfortable temperature, much like a natural incubator. This warmth can be especially important for babies in the NICU.

Supports breathing and heart rate

During skin-to-skin contact, many babies breathe more evenly and have steadier heart rates. The closeness and rhythm of your body can help your baby feel calm and regulated.

Encourages healthy growth and sleep

Babies held skin-to-skin often sleep more soundly. Restful sleep and reduced stress support healthy brain development and steady weight gain.

Supports your baby's immune system

Kangaroo Care can help protect your baby from stress and infection. Feeling safe and supported allows your baby's body to focus on healing and growing.

Kangaroo Care Helps You, Too!

Builds connection and bonding

Holding your baby close helps deepen your bond, even when words are not possible. These quiet moments of closeness are meaningful for both you and your baby.

Supports milk supply

For breastfeeding parents, skin-to-skin contact can encourage the body to produce more milk and support successful feeding.

Reduces stress and anxiety

Holding your baby releases calming hormones, such as oxytocin, which can help you feel more peaceful, confident, and connected during your NICU journey.

You Matter So Much

In the NICU, it's easy to feel like machines and monitors do all of the work, **but you are your baby's most powerful medicine.** Your touch, your smell, your voice—it all means the world to them. Kangaroo Care is more than a moment. It's a comfort; it's a gift – for both of you.

Additional Parent Resources

Printable guides, support groups, research/learning for parents, and so much more!

March of Dimes:
https://www.marchofdimes.org/our-work/nicu-family-support

Maternal Mental Health Leadership Alliance:
https://www.mmhla.org/nicu-resources-for-parents
(A comprehensive list of family support resources, including some of our personal favorites!)

NICU Connections:
https://nicuconnections.com

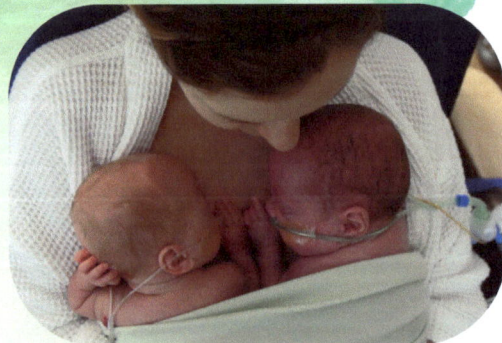

A Note from the Author

Dear Reader,

I was 25 weeks pregnant with our twin boys, Caleb and Owen, when I went into labor. At 26 weeks' gestation they burst into our world at 2lbs 1 oz and 1lb 13oz, respectively - and we were anything but ready. We spent 4 months in two different Neonatal Intensive Care Units, lived for a time at the Ronald McDonald House, juggled one twin coming home before the other, and ultimately spent those first days, months, and years in complete survival mode.

During our NICU admission, the hospital care team organized Kangaroo Care Week to educate and encourage parents. My husband, Jeremy, still laughs about the hairy-chested picture of he and our son that made it onto their promotional poster! While we sat with our boys, we would often read them picture books. It was during that time that Jeremy came up with the idea for *The Littlest Kangaroo*. He saw the need for a picture book that would allow parents not only to dream about the future, but also honor this temporary part of their journey.

It's been 10 years since Caleb and Owen inaugurated us into the NICU world, and while our boys' medical journeys have continued to evolve and challenge us ever since, they have also grown us as parents - and people - in ways we could have never fully realized without them. Every child, every parent, every family's NICU experience is different. We want you to know that however you're showing up for your baby right now, today, is enough.

For more resources and reflection, please visit us at our website:

Raisingspecialhumans.com
Email: Jen@Raisingspecialhumans.com

RAISING
special
HUMANS

ABOUT THE AUTHORS

Jen and Jeremy Moore are a husband-and-wife team from Dayton, Ohio, united by a shared commitment to leadership, education, healthcare, and family. *The Littlest Kangaroo* was inspired by their own journey as parents of twin boys, both of whom spent time in the NICU. Through this heartfelt story, they hope to celebrate the power of kangaroo care and bring comfort and encouragement to families walking a similar path.

Jeremy is an Emergency Medicine physician who has spent years caring for patients and families during life's most vulnerable moments. Jen is a dedicated teacher and writer who is passionate about helping children grow, learn, and feel authentically supported. Together they bring a unique blend of professional experience and personal perspective to this tale.

When they're not writing or working, the Moores enjoy family adventures with their twin boys, diving into a good book, taking walks with their miniature goldendoodle, and soaking up the small joys of family life.

ABOUT THE ILLUSTRATOR

Lola is an author, artist and life coach. She has three amazing children. Lola has published two poetry books and began her journey into the world of art a few years ago.

She is a strong advocate for her children, who all are autistic and have other conditions. Lola noted that kangaroo care was an important piece in all of her children's care.

Find Lola at :
lolalawrence0507@gmail.com
fb: Soul Collisions by Lola Lawrence

"For I know the plans I have for you," declares the Lord, "plans to prosper you and not harm you, plans to give you hope, and a future."

~ Jeremiah 29:11

"Be who you are and say what you feel, because those who mind don't matter and those who matter don't mind."
 - Dr. Seuss

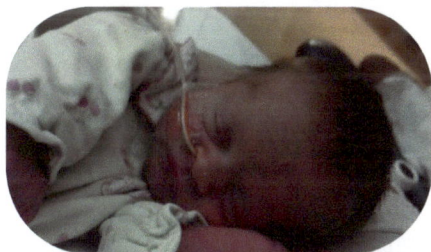

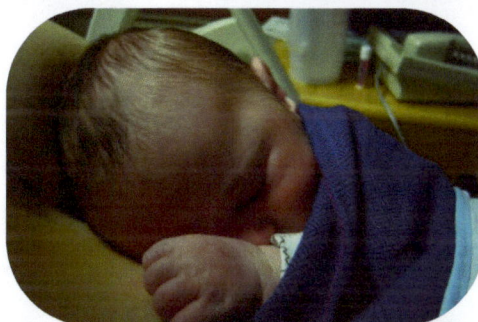
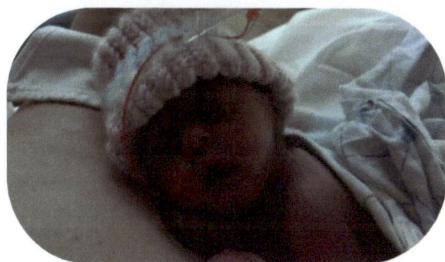

A nod to the research-based practice of Kangaroo Care, The Littlest Kangaroo is the perfect read-aloud for parents to enjoy with their babies during skin-to-skin care times.

All proceeds from the sale of The Littlest Kangaroo will be used to aid families in Neonatal Intensive Care Units nationwide, and is a perfect gift for those looking to support family and friends navigating their own NICU journeys.

www.ingramcontent.com/pod-product-compliance
Lightning Source LLC
Chambersburg PA
CBHW041429090426
42741CB00003B/101

* 9 7 9 8 9 9 9 9 2 1 3 6 0 0 *